NOAH'S and NAMAH'S ARK

NOAH'S and NAMAH'S ARK

by Charlotte Pomerantz
illustrated by Kelly K. M. Carson

Holt, Rinehart and Winston · New York

Library of Congress Cataloging in Publication Data
Pomerantz, Charlotte.   Noah's and Namah's ark.
Summary: Retells in rhyme the story of how Noah
and his family built the ark and saved the animals
from the Great Flood.
1. Noah's ark—Juvenile literature.   [1. Noah's ark.
2. Bible stories—O. T.]   I. Carson, Kelly K. M.
II. Title.   BS1238.N6P65   222'.1109505   80-14595
ISBN 0-03-057629-6

For John Lewis, a man like Noah   C. P.

To my friend and mentor, Zevi Moses Blum   K.C.

Noah quietly works the land.
God tells him of His anger
at the wickedness of man.

In the old old days there lived a man, Noah was his name.
He walked the earth in goodness in a time of greed and shame.
He plowed his narrow patch of land, not turning to look back.
The earth was fair, the hills were green, the soil was rich and
      black.

He was shooing away a fly, when the Lord appeared at his side.
"Good day to You, My Lord," he said. "Bad day," the Lord
      replied.
"True enough," said Noah. "These flies are a pesky lot."
"It's not the flies," said God. "It's the world; I like it not.
Mankind tears my heart in two, oh wicked, wretched race."
Noah stared; he'd never seen such anger on God's face.
"Man is violent," said God. "He vents his spleen by sword.
From Dan unto Beersheba, he disobeys the Lord.
I shall destroy him utterly—my pain is deep and dire."
"My Lord, what will You do?" said Noah. "Earthquake,
      plague, or fire?"
"No," said God. "I've pretty much decided on a flood.
Everything will disappear in water, waves, and mud."

In the eyes of God,
only one man is good—Noah.
He will save Noah and
his family.

"Every man will perish who has gone against my wishes,
Except for one good man—and innumerable fishes."
"Such a man," said Noah, "do I envy from the heart."
God sighed, "I made you good, all right, but maybe not
      too smart.
It's *you* I've chosen, Noah, from among all other men,
To begin the erring race of man all over once again."
Said Noah, "What of Namah, Lord, my good and faithful
      wife?"
"So be it," said the Lord. "I shall spare good Namah's life."
"And my three sons," said Noah, "worthy Japheth, Ham,
      and Shem."
"So be it," said the Lord. "I shall spare all three of them."
"And *their* three wives," said Noah, "whose names I do forget."
"So be it," said the Lord. "I'll see that none gets wet."
"And the great bearded uncle of Japheth's goodly wife?"
"Enough, already!" roared the Lord. "Enough—not one
      more life."

God tells Noah how to build
an ark to save himself and
his family from the flood.
Noah's wife Namah appears.

"But are You sure," said Noah, "that we won't perish too?"
"Don't worry," said the Lord. "I'll tell you what to do.
Cut down some cypress trees and build a mighty ark,
Strong enough to shelter you from flood and storm and dark.
Build it fifty cubits wide, three hundred cubits long.
Build it thirty cubits high—waterproof and strong."
Noah stared at the well-plowed land, then patted the
      old farm cat.
"I've never heard of a cubit," he said. "What, may I ask,
      is that?"
Then Namah, his pious wife, stepped forth. She'd been
      listening all the while.
"I can explain it to you," she said, with a warm and
      wifely smile.
"Noah," she said, "you're a man of God, but not too good
      at math.

A cubit is eighteen inches, my love—exactly a foot and a half.
The width of the ark is seventy feet; the length four hundred
and fifty.
The height of the boat to be forty-five. Noah, isn't that nifty?"
"Ma'am," said the Lord, "I'm much impressed with your
reason and multiplication."
"Good Sir," said Namah, "and I was impressed during the
whole of Creation.
Indeed, My Lord, You're a jack-of-all-trades, as well as a
Master of all."
The Lord blushed and sighed, "That was true enough,
Namah, up till the time of The Fall."

Noah asks Namah to help him build the ark. God tells them the ark must be big enough to hold two of every kind of animal.

"Dearest wife," said Noah, "you are worldly-wise and good.
Namah, will you help me build this mighty ship of wood?"
"Willingly," said Namah, "will I share this noble task.
In all things do we help each other. You need never ask."

She turned to God and said, "But I don't quite understand
Why we need so big a boat—so long, so wide, so grand?"
"You'll understand," said God, "when you hear what's on
    my mind.
For you will take the animals, two of every kind.

Of beasts and creepy-crawly things and birds of the air,
Of every creature on the earth, you will take a pair."

"I get it now," said Namah. "They'll enter two by two.
A ladybug, a man bug, two arctic caribou."
"Two cockatoos," said Noah. "Two katydids, two gnats."
"Two kangaroos," said Namah. "Two porcupines, two bats."
"A pair of swine," said Noah. "A sow, a bristly boar."
Said God, "Do not forget to build a window and a door."
"Two long-eared mutts," said Namah. "A male dog and a
      bitch."
"Be sure and seal the ark," said God, "inside and out with
      pitch."
"A nanny goat," said Namah, "and a billy goat gruff."
"You'd best begin the ark," said God. "The work is long
      and rough."
"A nanny goat," said Noah, "and a gruffy billy billy."
"Get on with it," said God. "You're beginning to sound silly."
"A flopsy and a mopsy, but no cottontail, boo hoo."
Then did the Lord crash down his fist and thunder,
      "That'll do!
I'll choose all the animals. You go build the ark.
Now set about your task at once. The hour grows late
      and dark."

*Noah, Namah, and their sons
and wives build the ark.*

Through desert heat, through wind and storm, through bitter
    aching cold,
The family of Noah labored, though he was five hundred
    years old.
One evening, having toiled for years, from morn till set of sun,
They cried to the Lord in one proud voice, "Come see the
    ark—it's done!"
Then Noah stood tall and called to the mountain, the prairie,
    the stones, and the air.
He called to the highland, the jungle, the tundra. He called,
    yes he called, everywhere.

Into Noah's Ark they came, two by two by two.
The doodlebugs dawdled and the cuckoo birds flew.
The bunny rabbits hopped and the wallabies jumped.
A goose got jostled and a bear got bumped.
Toothy alligators walked with bushy-tailed skunks,
Who walked behind two elephants, who walked behind their trunks.
Bat-faced foxes blinked at foxy-faced bats.
The bumblebees flew with the nightingales and gnats.
A shaggy-maned lion strolled with a lioness.
A saber-toothed tiger with a saber-toothed tigress.
The cheetahs raced ahead while the inchworms inched their way.
The rhinos moved along, but the hippos stopped to play.
Two frightened armadillos curled up tight into a ball.
Two fabled snow-white unicorns didn't show up at all.
Two humpèd camels strolled with one-hump dromedaries.
The hummingbirds flew with the terns and cassowaries.

Then Namah came along, chiding, "Your turn, gruffy billy.
And nanny, you are next in line. Get a move on, silly."

The ark is loaded with
provisions to last for a year.

When the family foregathered, they loaded the ark with
    provisions to last for a year.
Flour and salt, barley and malt, cider and sheep's milk
    and beer.
Coarse oatmeal porridge, animal forage, olives and fruits
    of the vine.
Flat bread and cheese, honey from bees, melons and
    pomegranate wine.
All kinds of spices and cooking devices: grinders and clay
    pots and bowls.
Rolling pins, cookie tins, ladles and dreidels, bagels and
    poppy-seed rolls.
Flavory, savory, chewy and gooey, mooshy and squooshy
    delights
For the beasts of the field, the birds of the air, and the
    humans on long rainy nights.
And they didn't forget the cranchy, craunchy, crunchy
    buckwheat groats
For the fluffy nanny nanny and the gruffy billy goats.

*When all are safe within
the ark, the flood begins.*

As soon as all had entered through the ark's wide door,
Lightning flashed, thunder rolled, the rain began to pour.
Then were the fountains of the deep crashed open.
Then were the windows of the sky smashed, broken.
Then did it rain for forty days and forty nights.
Then did the waters rise to terrifying heights.
The highest hills were swallowed up, but still God did not stop
Till nothing could be seen—not the tallest mountaintop.
As far as His eye reached, there was water, nothing more.
The earth was now a roaring sea—a sea without a shore.

God remembers Noah and ends the rain.
The floodwaters finally abate and the
ark comes to rest on Mount Ararat.

Then one day Noah looked about and cried, "The rains have
     ended!
Our ark sails over mountains, between sea and sky suspended."
"It's true enough," said Namah. "The seas have raised
     the ark.
But *ai,* the earth we knew and loved is steeped in watery dark."
The waters kept on going down, and sometime after that,
The great ark came to rest atop the Mount of Ararat.
They'd been ten months on the boat when they all looked out
     and cheered;
For above the shrinking seas, other mountaintops appeared.
From deep within the crowded ark came soothing sounds
     and sighs:
Squirrels churring, pumas purring, wordless lullabies.
They could hear the zebra braying, the mare and stallion
     neighing,
And in the hush of night, they could hear the mantis praying.
They could hear the love doves cooing, the friendly
     moo-cow mooing,
And well they could imagine what everyone was doing.

Namah sends for the dove to go forth and look for dry land. On the second day, the dove returns with a freshly plucked olive leaf in her beak.

Namah sent for the dove and said, "This day you must fly
    from here,
And return to tell if the earth is green; whether dry land
    is near."
The dove flew away and was gone all day, but came back to
    the ark that night.
She floated down to the window ledge, a weary and pitiful
    sight.
"Don't leave the ark," the little bird warned. "Floodwaters
    surge all around.
Nowhere at all did I find a spot to rest my feet on dry ground."
Namah reached out to the weary dove and carried her
    gently inside.
"Ah me, I sent you too early," she said. "Ah me," said
    the dove, and sighed.
When seven days passed, she said to the dove, "Once more
    must you fly from here.
Try, little dove, to bring one sign of hope. One hint that
    dry land is near."
In evening calm, the dove returned, a fresh olive leaf in
    her beak.

Noah gathered her into his arms and held her against his
cheek.

"Lo," cooed the dove, "I bring you good tidings. Olive and
fig trees abound.

And everywhere green fields and pasturelands rise from
the still sodden ground."

"His gracious will be done and praised," said Namah to
the dove.

"You bring us proof of God's green earth, His mercy and
His love."

Noah wept, for he had seen the anger on God's face.

But now he felt His goodness, His all-supporting grace.

When Noah lifts the roof of the ark
on New Year's Day, the earth is dry.
God makes His covenant—a rainbow.
This is the promise between God and earth.

On New Year's Day, Noah lifted the roof and cried out,
  "Namah, behold!
Mountains and valleys, forests and meadows, just as the dove
  had foretold."
Then the voice of the Lord was heard by all who waited
  within the ark:
"Never again will I drown the living world in watery dark.
Listen to my covenant, my promise unto you,
And all the generations that shall fill the world anew:
While the earth remains, seedtime, harvest, heat and cold,
Summer, winter, day and night shall ever more unfold.
Look up, my friends, look up," said God; His voice was
  kingly proud.

"Behold my covenant to you—a rainbow in a cloud.
For as the fresh green olive leaf is proof of a new birth,
So the rainbow signifies my promise to the earth.
And now," said God, "the time has come for all to leave
  the ark.
To feel the sunlight on your backs; forget the months of dark."

The animals
leave the ark.

Down the mountainside they came in little groups of threes:
Three meadowlarks, three cuckoo birds, three snakes, three bumblebees.
Three doodlebugs dawdled, three wallabies jumped.
A gosling got jostled, a bear cub got bumped.
Three toothy alligators walked behind three bushy skunks,
Who walked behind three elephants, who walked behind their trunks.
Bat-faced foxes blinked at foxy-faced bats.
The hummingbirds flew with the nightingales and gnats.
The lion and the lion cub strolled with the lioness.
The tiger and his cub with the saber-toothed tigress.

Three cheetahs raced ahead, while the inchworms inched their way.
The rhinos moved along, but the hippos stopped to play.
There were three two-humpèd camels, three one-hump dromedaries.
Above them flew three butterflies, three terns, three cassowaries.
A frightened armadillo baby curled up in a ball;
And for awhile no one could find him anywhere at all.
The dove flew with her doveling, the green leaf in her beak.
Her mate cooed, "Such a pretty world! Come and take a peek."
"The sea," said the doveling, "is the sea as wide and blue?"
"Indeed," two puffins nodded, "and all of it's for you."

At the very very end of the line to leave the boat
Were a nanny and a billy and a little Willy goat.
Said the gruffy billy billy to the fluffy nanny nanny,
"When Willy has a kid, then you'll be Granny Nanny."
"And you," said nanny nanny, "will be gruffy Grandpa Billy."
"Oh look," a woman's voice cried out. "Just look at little
    Willy!"
Namah clapped her hands and chuckled, "Now we have
    three goats."
"Meh," said little Willy, "crunchy munchy buckwheat groats."

Then Noah kissed his wife and said, "My dear and loving
    Namah,
It looks to me as if you are about to be a mama."
"And what of us?" called out the wives of Japheth, Ham
    and Shem.
Then did the three sons shout for joy, "Oh, Good Lord,
    look at them!"

*And Noah lived after the flood 350 years.
And all the days of Noah were 950 years:
and he died.*

*From Noah and Namah and their sons and
their sons' wives was the whole world
peopled. From Billy, Nanny, Willy, and all
the animals was the whole world animaled.*

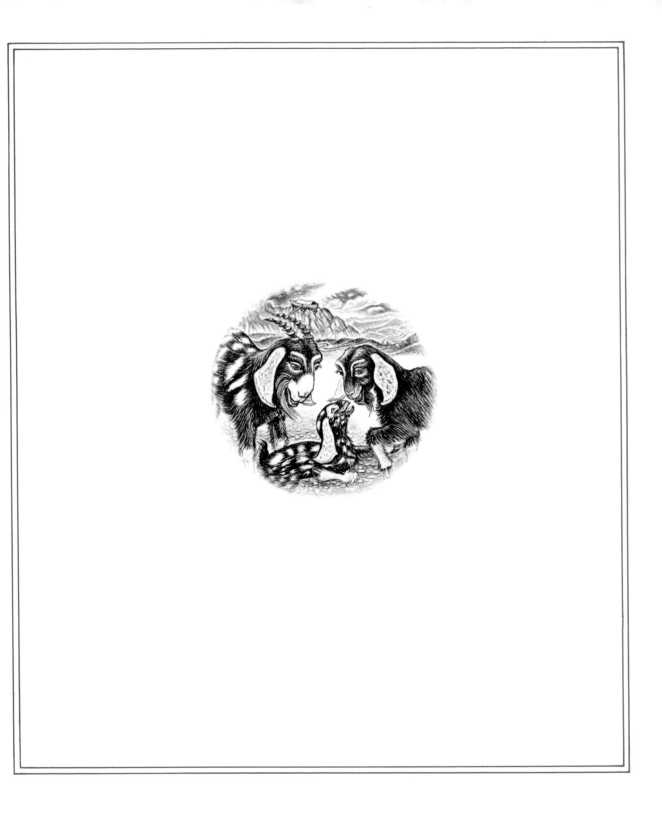

About the Author

Charlotte Pomerantz has written more than a dozen books for children as well as *Eureka!,* a play about Archimedes. Her book, *The Princess and the Admiral,* won the Jane Addams Children's Book Award for "its contribution to the dignity and equality of all mankind." Ms. Pomerantz lives in New York City with her husband who is also a writer.

About the Illustrator

Kelly K. M. Carson grew up on the shores of Lake Ontario in Wilson, New York, graduated from Cornell with a Bachelor of Science degree in Floriculture and Ornamental Horticulture. She took architectural history and design courses at Columbia University in New York City, and studied at the Art Student's League.